IMAGES
of America

WALDORF ASTORIA

IMAGES
of America

WALDORF ASTORIA

William Alan Morrison

ARCADIA
PUBLISHING

Copyright © 2014 by William Alan Morrison
ISBN 978-1-4671-2128-6

Published by Arcadia Publishing
Charleston, South Carolina

Printed in the United States of America

Library of Congress Control Number: 2013946820

For all general information, please contact Arcadia Publishing:
Telephone 843-853-2070
Fax 843-853-0044
E-mail sales@arcadiapublishing.com
For customer service and orders:
Toll-Free 1-888-313-2665

Visit us on the Internet at www.arcadiapublishing.com

To my parents, James Alan and Anne Diemer Morrison,
who celebrated their wedding reception at the
Waldorf Astoria on August 12, 1938.

CONTENTS

ACKNOWLEDGMENTS

A book of this kind could not exist without the generous cooperation and assistance of others. The author would like to express his sincere gratitude to the Waldorf Astoria Archives, especially to its archivist, Erin Allsop, for providing many of the images that appear in this book. Thanks are also due to John J. Blazejewski, photographer at the Princeton University Library, for recreating images from *The Waldorf-Astoria, New York*, originally published by Waldorf-Astoria proprietor George C. Boldt and photographer Benjamin Falke in 1902. The Prints & Photographs Division of the Library of Congress duplicated many photographs of people, places, and events associated with both Waldorf Astorias, and the Avery Architectural Archives at Columbia University provided a visual record of the demolition of the first Waldorf-Astoria in 1929. Individual photographs or drawings provided by the above institutions are credited throughout the book. Images without a courtesy line come from the author's personal collection.

The author would also like to express his thanks to his son George S. Morrison, who, despite the fact that his interests lie more with *Grand Theft Auto* than with grand hotels, proofread much of this book and was of constant aid to his prehistoric father in dealing with uncooperative computer programs.

INTRODUCTION

In sheer terms of its name, New York City's Waldorf Astoria may well be the best-known hotel in the world. Synonymous with grandeur, luxury, and sophistication, its name has been appropriated by numerous imposter hotels from London to Shanghai, by the Waldorf's own ubiquitous salad, and somewhat amusingly, by one of Jim Henson's Muppets. The Waldorf Astoria has been celebrated (and occasionally excoriated) in both song and verse by such talents as Irving Berlin, Langston Hughes, Cole Porter, Wallace Stevens, and Thomas E. "Fats" Waller. It has been featured in countless books, plays, and movies, including a top-billed role in MGM's 1945 melodrama *Weekend at the Waldorf*. Thousands of people who have never set foot through its doors know the Waldorf Astoria by sight and reputation.

The Waldorf Astoria has been the subject of at least a dozen separate books, which relate its colorful history in rich, and sometimes lurid, prose. This book intends to be more of a visual record, a sort of family album, if you will, of this grandest of grand hotels, but in order to proceed, certain facts must be highlighted.

To begin with, there was not one New York hotel called the Waldorf Astoria, but two, and some might say even three. The first Waldorf-Astoria (its name properly hyphenated) resulted from the union of two separate hotels, the Waldorf and the Astoria, built next door to each other on Fifth Avenue during the Gilded Age of the 1890s. Conceived as a civic palace embodying the wealth and position New York City had achieved by the end of the 19th century, it revolutionized America's idea of what a hotel could be and stimulated the building of scores of palatial hotels in cities across the nation emulating its regal ambitions. This first Waldorf-Astoria was demolished in 1929.

The second Waldorf Astoria (without the hyphen) is the present establishment located at Park Avenue and East Forty-ninth Street. Opened in 1931, it was the largest, the tallest, and the most expensive hotel that had ever been built, not just succeeding its illustrious predecessor, but surpassing it in every way imaginable. Today, more than 80 years after its completion, the Waldorf Astoria remains the epitome of the grand hotel.

Hotels and their colonial antecedents, inns and taverns, have played a prominent role in American history since before the country's founding. In 1776, members of the Second Continental Congress were fed and housed in Philadelphia's inns and taverns, likely discussing Thomas Jefferson's controversial declaration over a tankard of ale and plate of terrapin stew. Pres. George Washington, members of his cabinet, and ministers from foreign nations danced at cotillions honoring his birthday in 1792, 1793, and 1794. During the early years of the 19th century, the city hotel grew rapidly in both size and stature. In 1836, John Jacob Astor, whose descendants would play a prominent role in the creation of the first Waldorf-Astoria, built New York's first true luxury hotel, the 300-room Astor House on Broadway, opposite the New York City Hall. One of the first American buildings illuminated by gaslight and featuring indoor plumbing, the Astor House served as New York City's social and cultural center for a number of years, hosting Henry

Wadsworth Longfellow, Jenny Lind, Henry Clay, and Abraham Lincoln within its white granite walls. The year 1859 brought the Fifth Avenue Hotel on Madison Square, the first American hotel to boast an elevator, private bathrooms, and enough gilt and plush velvet to impress even the visiting prince of Wales.

Post–Civil War New York hotels were an entirely different matter. Largely male domains, they primarily served as permanent residences for confirmed bachelors and as stopovers for traveling salesmen who displayed their wares in the hotel's sample rooms. Spread up and down Broadway, their chief source of revenue was inevitably a saloon, where free lunch counters and long brass-railed bars attracted crowds of cigar-smoking political bosses, ward healers, and favor-seekers, all talking business, sports, or politics. The only women on the premises were barmaids and waitresses, often subjected to off-color remarks or unwelcome advances from their boisterous, masculine clientele. A handful of the better establishments offered ladies' dining rooms for women accompanied by a male escort. Respectable male citizens of New York seldom patronized the Broadway hostelries and respectable women not at all. At many establishments, an unescorted young woman seen hanging about a hotel exchange for any length of time was usually assumed to be a prostitute and given the bum's rush by the house detective. Such actions were not taken to protect the hotel's reputation, as the hotel porter often provided male guests arriving at even the most fashionable New York hotels with a printed list of first-class brothels found in the vicinity, a service for which the hotel proprietor was handsomely reimbursed.

New York's late-19th-century hotels were particularly shunned by the well-to-do aristocrats who made up the city's vaunted "Four Hundred." Dwelling in an aloof conclave of wealth, privilege, and pedigree far removed from the rough and tumble city around them, they attended private banquets, private receptions, and private balls in private Fifth Avenue mansions or members-only clubs. When events such as the annual charity ball required larger quarters, an armory would be rented and admission granted by invitation only. The thought of holding such festivities amid the raucous ballyhoo of a Broadway hotel would have been unthinkable.

Until the Waldorf came along, that is . . .

Set in the very heart of the fashionable Fifth Avenue residential district, the new hotel was intended to specifically cater to the socially prominent ladies and gentlemen of New York and the increasing number of distinguished foreign visitors to the city from abroad. To them, the Waldorf proffered the finest in French cuisine, a telephone in every room, and the privacy of meals served in their chambers—the first room service. It surrounded them with the art and trappings of a European royal court and an army of servants seeing to their every wish. Clearly, the Waldorf was *their* hotel.

And how did all this come about? It began as a tale of two cousins.

One

A Fit Place
for a Gentleman

At 16 years old, John Jacob Astor emigrated from the small German village of Waldorf, where he had been born and raised, to the newly independent United States in 1779. Here, he amassed a sizable fortune as a fur trader in the Oregon Territory and later as the purchaser of large tracts of real estate on the island of Manhattan. By the time of his death in 1848, with an estate estimated at over $20 million, Astor was reckoned to be America's richest man. Forty years of prudent management by his son and grandsons increased the value of the Astor estate to over $200 million.

In 1890, the principal heirs to the Astor fortune were John Jacob Astor's two great-grandsons, 41-year-old William Waldorf Astor and his 25-year-old cousin John Jacob Astor IV, who lived next door to each other in substantial Fifth Avenue mansions at either end of the block between Thirty-third and Thirty-fourth Streets. Between the two Astor houses lay a walled private garden and a turgid sea of mutual dislike. The eldest son of his generation, the imperious William Waldorf Astor viewed himself as the family's natural head and director of its immense real estate empire. He despised his cousin as an indolent loafer and greatly resented his aunt's position as "queen" of New York society. Creator of the Four Hundred, a who's who of the social elite in New York City, Caroline Schermerhorn Astor reigned supreme as *the* Mrs. Astor, a title William Waldorf believed rightly belonged to his wife. For years, he waged a dogged campaign to wrest his aunt from her august throne, but to his chagrin, no one in society chose to take his side against the powerful Caroline Astor. Declaring that "America was not a fit place for a gentleman to live," an embittered William Waldorf Astor announced that he and his family would move to England, permanently. As a parting barrage at his aunt and cousin, he further noted that his Thirty-third Street mansion would be demolished and replaced by a multistory hotel—a hotel that would be known as the Waldorf.

DRAWING OF THE HOTEL WALDORF. Pictured is the display of the West Thirty-third Street frontage. (Courtesy of Princeton University Library.)

HOTEL WALDORF FROM ACROSS FIFTH AVENUE. "This hotel is a palace," proclaimed the *New York Times* prior to the opening of the Hotel Waldorf on March 2, 1893. Designed by architect Henry J. Hardenbergh in an ebullient German Renaissance style, the 14-story Waldorf towered over the staid brownstone residences of its surrounding neighborhood. With a frontage of 100 feet on Fifth Avenue and 250 feet on West Thirty-third Street, its lofty stone-and-brick exterior was animated by an effusion of balconies, alcoves, arcades, and loggias beneath a tile roof bedecked with gables and turrets. (Courtesy of Waldorf Astoria Archives and Library of Congress.)

WILLIAM WALDORF ASTOR (1848–1919). The most intelligent and ambitious of his Astor generation, if also "a very prickly sort of person," William Waldorf Astor had trained as a lawyer at Harvard and pursued a political career by serving in the New York State Assembly and Senate. Defeated twice when he ran for Congress (losses he greatly resented), Astor was appointed US ambassador to Italy by Pres. Chester Arthur. He developed a passionate interest in Italian art and culture, which he displayed in two historical romance novels he wrote before being recalled to America when Grover Cleveland became president. After his move to England, Astor became a British citizen and devoted a large portion of his fortune to the purchase and restoration of Cliveden and Hever Castle, two classic English country houses. In London, he purchased the *Pall Mall Gazette* newspaper and built the still-operating Hotel Waldorf in the city's West End. Through his business enterprises and numerous large donations to English charities, Astor eventually gained a title, viscount of Hever, and a seat in the House of Lords. Though he seldom returned to America and never visited the hotel he had built on the site of his boyhood home, Astor continued to manage his New York real estate holdings, building the Hotel Astor in 1904 and stimulating the development of Times Square as a theater and entertainment district. (Courtesy of King's Notable New Yorkers, 1896–1899.)

MAIN ENTRANCE TO THE HOTEL WALDORF. Sheltered by an elaborate frosted-glass-and-wrought-iron marquee, this entrance on West Thirty-third Street led directly to the hotel's registration desk. Public areas occupied the whole of the Waldorf's double-height ground-floor level, with its 450 guest rooms and 350 baths spanning the eight stories above. An additional 100 sleeping rooms for servants and the hotel's laundry filled the four floors directly under its roof. (Courtesy of Princeton University Library.)

ENTRANCE HALL AND REGISTRATION DESK. Finished in Sienna marble with a coffered ceiling and a mosaic tile floor, the Waldorf's entrance hall provided an impressive foyer to the hotel's major public rooms. When the Astoria opened in 1897, the Waldorf's registration desk became a newsstand. (Courtesy of Library of Congress.)

MAIN CORRIDOR AND STAIRCASE. Off the main corridor leading to the Empire Room was an alcove containing three guest elevators and a grand staircase leading to mezzanine-level shops, reception rooms, and the hotel's executive offices. (Courtesy of *Harper's* magazine.)

MARIE ANTOINETTE SALON. A replica of a room in the Louvre, this oval women's reception room was furnished with 18th-century French antiques and reproductions that Boldt and his wife had selected on their 1892 European buying trip. Also featured were a marble bust of Marie Antoinette, an antique clock once owned by her, and a ceiling mural by artist Will H. Low titled *The Birth of Venus*. (Courtesy of Princeton University Library.)

EMPIRE ROOM RESTAURANT. With walls paneled in carved Honduran mahogany and green silk brocade, ornamented ceilings painted by the Crowningshield firm of Boston, and two phalanxes of polished black marble columns, the Empire Room was both the largest and most elaborately decorated of the Waldorf's public rooms. Within months of its opening, the Empire Room joined Delmonico's and Sherry's as one of the most favored restaurants among affluent New Yorkers. (Courtesy of Princeton University Library.)

EMPIRE ROOM FIREPLACE. Located on the Empire Room's north wall, the fireplace typifies architect Hardenbergh's florid design style. (Courtesy of Princeton University Library.)

WALDORF GENTLEMEN'S CAFÉ. As its robust black oak paneling, hunting murals, and stag-horn chandeliers suggest, this was an exclusively masculine domain. Boldt, however, decreed that the room would have no brass-railed bar and that its patrons would be served their libations only while seated at tables, a decision that did not sit well with some saloon old-timers. (Courtesy of Princeton University Library.)

GENTLEMEN'S CAFÉ DECOR. Architect Henry J. Hardenbergh's watercolor drawing of the wall treatment in the Gentlemen's Café illustrates the extent to which he was responsible for the Waldorf's interior decor as well as its architectural design. (Courtesy of Princeton University Library.)

WALDORF PALM GARDEN. Directly opposite the hotel's main entrance, the Palm Garden was a novel feature that, previously unknown in America, Boldt had seen in European hotels. Intended as a space to which men and women might retire together after dinner, it instead gained instant popularity as a place for society women to meet for luncheons or afternoon tea. (Courtesy of Princeton University Library.)

TURKISH SALON. Decorated by the Herter Brothers firm as a carved teak and sandalwood evocation of the Ottoman Empire, the Turkish Salon served as a men's-only smoking room. Arabic quotations from the Koran decorated the room's upper walls as did, somewhat incongruously, a sword once owned by Napoleon I. (Courtesy of Princeton University Library.)

PORTRAIT OF GEORGE C. BOLDT (1851–1918). Hailed at his death as "the most famous hotelman in the world," George Boldt was born on the Baltic Sea island of Rugen and came to New York at the age of 13, finding his first employment as a restaurant dishwasher. Over the next 25 years, he gained experience in every facet of hotel operation and served as assistant manager and maître d' of the prestigious Philadelphia Club, the nation's oldest and most exclusive gentlemen's social organization. In 1880, newly married and backed financially by the Philadelphia Club's affluent members, Boldt went into business for himself as proprietor of the Bellevue Hotel, which he made Philadelphia's preeminent dining establishment and a fashionable resort for the city's wealthy elite. Ten years later, he was asked to become the proprietor of the proposed Hotel Waldorf. Declaring "We must make this hotel a haven for the well-to-do," Boldt transformed the role of the American hotel from temporary housing for out-of-town visitors to that of a social and civic center for the entire city. At both the Waldorf-Astoria and the Bellevue-Stratford Hotel, which he opened in Philadelphia in 1904, George Boldt created municipal palaces that became the centers of social activity for their respective cities. Today, he is less well known as the creator of the modern American hotel than as the owner/builder of Boldt's Castle, his summer home in New York's Thousand Islands, which Boldt left unfinished following the death of his wife in 1904. (Courtesy of Waldorf Astoria Archives.)

THE FIRST WALDORF BALLROOM. In an era when most balls were still held in private homes, George Boldt's aspiration to make the Waldorf ballroom a focus of New York social life was certainly an uncertain proposition. Yet it became just that the night the Waldorf opened with a charity event, hosted by Alva Vanderbilt, that featured the New York Philharmonic. With its own separate entrance from Thirty-third Street and a mezzanine level boasting private reception rooms, banquet halls, and a musician's gallery (shown here), the charming green-and-gold Waldorf ballroom was entirely shut off from the rest of the hotel, giving it an aura of aloof exclusivity most appealing to its elite patronage. (Courtesy of Princeton University Library.)

THE BRADLEY MARTIN BALLROOM. The extreme popularity of the Waldorf ballroom led Boldt to plan for a significantly larger replacement. In the fall of 1896, the Waldorf received a four-story addition to its western end, which contained a new 3,800-square-foot ballroom—more than four times the size of its predecessor. Only a few months after its opening, this new facility was the site of the infamous Bradley Martin costume ball, the million-dollar-plus price tag of which incensed newspaper editorial writers and crusading clerics across a nation suffering from recession and widespread unemployment. So virulent was the public's outrage that the ball's profligate sponsors fled to Europe for their safety. In a matter of months, the even grander Astoria ballroom superseded this second Waldorf ballroom. (Courtesy of Princeton University Library.)

HENRY IV DRAWING ROOM, WALDORF STATE APARTMENTS. Located on the second floor straddling the Waldorf's Fifth Avenue and Thirty-third Street corner, the State Apartments was a suite of nine rooms intended for visiting foreign dignitaries. Its decor mingled 16th- and 17th-century French and Italian antiques and tapestries that George Boldt and his wife had purchased in Europe, along with reproductions fashioned by the W. & J. Sloane Company. Its first notable occupant was Princess Eulalie, the Spanish infanta, who was passing through New York on her way to Chicago, where she would be her country's official representative at the World's Columbian Exposition. (Courtesy of Princeton University Library.)

FRANCOIS V BEDROOM, WALDORF STATE APARTMENTS. This elaborate bedstead, an American reproduction of an original at the Palais de Fontainebleau, was occupied by a parade of notables, including Chinese viceroy Li Hung-Chang; Chowfa Maha Rajiravuth, the crown prince of Siam; and Albert of Saxe-Coburg, king of the Belgians, who was less taken with the suite's decor than with its telephones. (Courtesy of Princeton University Library.)

MUSIC ROOM AND DUCHESS BEDROOM, WALDORF STATE APARTMENTS. The State Apartments' major rooms were intended to vie in opulence with those of the most extravagant Fifth Avenue mansions. Interestingly, more than one of the suite's guests offered to buy its contents for installation in their own homes. (Courtesy of Princeton University Library.)

BANQUET HALL, WALDORF STATE APARTMENTS. Capable of seating 20 at dinner, the walls of the State Suite's private dining room displayed George Boldt's personal china collection, including 48 Sevres plates painted with portraits of European royalty he had commissioned especially for this room. (Courtesy of Princeton University Library.)

LI HUNG-CHANG. Few visitors to the city have ever aroused the fascination of New Yorkers like Chinese viceroy Li Hung-Chang, the combination prime minister, foreign minister, commander of the Chinese Army, and lord high admiral of its navy. Passing through the city in 1896 on his return to China from attending the coronation of Czar Nicholas II of Russia, the silk-garbed mandarin traveled with an entourage of 18 aides, 22 servants, 300 pieces of luggage, several cages of songbirds and parrots, and a plentiful supply of 100-year-old eggs. Escorted into New York Harbor by a fleet of US Navy battleships and through the streets of Manhattan by a regiment of US cavalry, he drew crowds of curious onlookers and barrages of firecrackers everywhere he went in a golden sedan chair borne by four servants. To welcome Li Hung-Chang to the Waldorf, George Boldt had silken dragon banners and Chinese lanterns displayed throughout the hotel and a giant Imperial Chinese flag flown on the Fifth Avenue flagstaff. (Courtesy of Waldorf Astoria Archives.)

ASTOR DINING ROOM. Perhaps the most curious of the Waldorf's private banquet rooms was the installation of the family dining room from the demolished Astor mansion. Three stories above its original site, the room was faithfully recreated, from the original paneling, drapery, carpeting, and fireplace mantel to the Astor family china and silverware on the table. The only change was to the lighting fixtures; originally oil burning, they were wired for electricity. (Courtesy of Princeton University Library.)

ASTOR RECEPTION ROOM. Though not part of the original Astor mansion, the reception room contained many pieces of furniture from the razed house, which William Waldorf Astor chose to leave behind on his move to London. (Courtesy of Princeton University Library.)

Two

MEET ME AT THE HYPHEN

Reaction to the new Hotel Waldorf was not universally favorable. Dismissing his cousin's new hostelry as a "glorified tavern," John Jacob Astor IV announced that he would demolish his own mansion adjacent to the Waldorf and replace it with New York's largest livery stable. Cooler heads soon prevailed, however, and the Astor Estate, with the aid of George Boldt, was able to convince the young multimillionaire that a more fitting use of such valuable real estate would be for John Jacob Astor IV to build a hotel of his own, one that would be bigger and grander than the parvenu Waldorf in every way. After long and occasionally contentious negotiations between the English and American Astors, it was agreed that the Waldorf and the new hotel would be interconnected and that George Boldt would serve as proprietor of both. However, it was also stipulated in the contracts for the new building that, should conflict arise again between the Astor cousins, the corridors connecting their two hotels would be sealed off and the properties operated as separate enterprises. A further condition of the contract stated that whenever the names of the two hotels appeared jointly in print, they must be separated by a hyphen to underscore the tenuous nature of their union. The Astor mansion and seven adjacent Astor-owned townhouses were demolished in May 1895, and ground was broken for the new hotel the following month. Plans were also made for Astor Court, a private 200-foot-long thoroughfare between Thirty-third and Thirty-fourth Streets, just west of the combined hotels, which would provide them with street frontages on all four sides. Only one issue remained unresolved between the two Astor cousins: what would the new hotel be called? John Jacob Astor wanted it named the Schermerhorn after his mother, the formidable queen of New York society, Caroline Schermerhorn Astor. William Waldorf Astor would not tolerate such an honor being bestowed upon his onetime bitter adversary. Finally, just a few months before the new hotel was to open, the two Astor cousins agreed to call it the Astoria, after the fur-trading outpost the first John Jacob Astor had established at the mouth of Oregon's Columbia River in 1811.

JOHN JACOB ASTOR IV MANSION AND THE HOTEL WALDORF. The brownstone mansion at Fifth Avenue and Thirty-fourth Street where John Jacob Astor IV lived with his family and mother crouches in the looming shadow of the "glorified tavern" built by his expatriate cousin. Soon, the remaining Astors would depart for a new residence at Fifth Avenue and Sixty-fifth Street, and their Thirty-fourth Street mansion would be razed for the site of the Astoria. (Courtesy of Waldorf Astoria Archives.)

WALDORF-ASTORIA FROM EAST THIRTY-FOURTH STREET. Architect Henry Hardenbergh returned to design the bigger, grander Astoria, a task he fulfilled with considerable aplomb. Rising to a height of 18 stories and stretching 350 feet along West Thirty-fourth Street, it reduced the neighboring Waldorf to the status of poor relation. A mammoth cliff of dark red brick topped by a three-story mansard roof, the new Astoria dominated the view for blocks up and down Fifth Avenue, its sheer magnitude setting a new standard for grand hotels of the coming century. (Courtesy of Library of Congress.)

WALDORF-ASTORIA FROM THE ROOF OF THE B. ALTMAN DEPARTMENT STORE. The first three floors of the Astoria were given over almost entirely to restaurants, banquet rooms, and ballrooms. The next 12 floors consisted of 550 guest rooms and suites, with the remaining space beneath the roof reserved for service facilities. Atop the building was New York's loftiest open-air roof garden. Their combined room count made the Waldorf-Astoria far and away the city's—and America's—largest hotel. (Courtesy of Library of Congress.)

John Jacob Astor IV (1864–1912). Shy, inarticulate, and rather awkward, John Jacob Astor IV took no role in the operation of the Astor Estate Office or any other profession. Devoted to his mother, he entered, at her urging, a socially impeccable but loveless marriage to Philadelphia aristocrat Ava Willing, who treated both him and their son Vincent with ill-concealed contempt. A great deal of his time was spent at his country house near Rhinebeck, New York, where he tinkered with inventions or cruised on his private yacht. Widely viewed by the New York press as an aimless dilettante—one newspaper periodically referring to him in print as "Jack Ass-tor"—his reputation improved after the opening of the Astoria and his subsequent building of Fifth Avenue's Hotel St. Regis and the Knickerbocker Hotel at Broadway and Forty-second Street. Following his mother's death in 1908, Astor and his wife were divorced amid much rancor and scandal. In 1911, he married Madeleine Force, a woman 17 years his junior, and embarked upon a long honeymoon in Europe and the Middle East. Planning to return to New York in April 1912, Astor and his wife booked passage on the ill-fated White Star liner RMS *Titanic*. Madeleine Force Astor and their unborn son survived the tragedy; John Jacob Astor IV did not. (Courtesy of King's Notable New Yorkers, 1896–1899.)

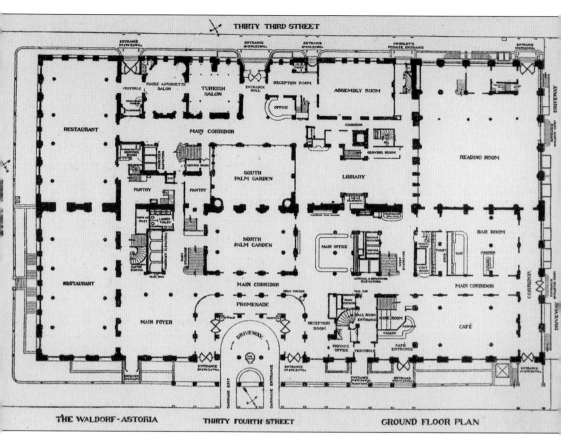

WALDORF-ASTORIA MAIN FLOOR PLAN. John Jacob Astor IV might have stipulated that connecting links between the Waldorf and the Astoria be kept to a minimum so that they could be easily separated from each other, but George Boldt's operational scheme for the hyphenated hostelry made a divorce highly unlikely. When the Astoria opened, the Waldorf's Gentlemen's Café was turned into a library and the Bradley Martin Ballroom became a reading and game room. The Waldorf's Palm Garden was merged with that of the Astoria, and the two Fifth Avenue restaurants were connected to each other as well. In the end, only the hyphen in the Waldorf-Astoria's name endured to suggest that they might have been conceived as two separate entities. (Courtesy of Princeton University Library.)

HENRY J. HARDENBERGH (1847–1918). Already well known as the architect of New York's 1884 Dakota Apartments, Henry Hardenbergh's design for the Waldorf-Astoria embarked him on a new career as America's premiere architect of grand hotels, among them the Manhattan (1896), Plaza (1907), and Martinique (1911) Hotels in New York; the Copley Plaza Hotel (1912) in Boston; the New Willard (1901) and Raleigh (1911) Hotels in Washington, DC; and the Windsor Hotel Annex (1907) in Montreal, Canada. His non-hotel work included a library and a chapel for Rutgers College, of which Hardenbergh's great-great-grandfather had been a founder and first president, and Princeton University's original Palmer Stadium. Several of Hardenbergh's surviving buildings have been designated as New York City Landmarks. (Courtesy of King's Notable New Yorkers, 1896–1899.)

ASTORIA CARRIAGE ENTRANCE. Surrounded by a glass-enclosed promenade for pedestrians, a U-shaped carriage drive for horse-drawn hansom cabs entered the Astoria from Thirty-fourth Street, along with three other entrances that led to the hotel's restaurant, ballroom, and men's café, respectively. (Courtesy of Princeton University Library.)

ASTORIA FOYER LOUNGE. Just inside the Thirty-fourth Street carriage entrance was a foyer lounge with seating for 60, a pair of marble statues, a hooded fireplace, and an ornate four-sided bronze clock, created by the Goldsmiths' Company of London for exhibition at the 1893 Chicago World's Fair and purchased by George Boldt at the fair's closing. With the exception of the summer months, the foyer lounge offered free concerts by the hotel's string ensemble each evening. (Courtesy of Princeton University Library and Waldorf Astoria Archives.)

WALDORF-ASTORIA REGISTRATION DESK. Beyond the foyer lounge was the marble and tooled bronze registration desk. Here were combined check-in facilities, the hotel cashier and accounting offices, and the mail and information desk for guests of both the Waldorf and the Astoria. Behind the registration desk was a handsome glass and mahogany enclosure—purportedly the nation's first long-distance telephone booth—as well as a pneumatic tube system for delivering calling cards and messages to the guest rooms. (Courtesy of Princeton University Library.)

ASTORIA PALM GARDEN. Of this room George Boldt once remarked, "I'd rather see Mrs. Stuyvesant Fish enjoying a cup of tea in an all but empty Palm Garden than a dozen lesser-known guests there feasting." Deemed by many to be the most exclusive dining venue in New York, entry to the Astoria's palm-filled social Valhalla was rigidly guarded by the ever-vigilant "Oscar of the Waldorf" (maître d' Oscar Tschirky) and his velvet rope. Surrounded by three stories of arcaded balconies with an overhead skylight, it became the preferred setting for Mamie Fish and her blue book sisters to retire after a hectic day of shopping along Sixth Avenue's Ladies' Mile. (Courtesy of Princeton University Library.)

ROSE ROOM RESTAURANT. Like the Waldorf's Empire Room, the Astoria's principal restaurant occupied the whole of the hotel's east side frontage overlooking Fifth Avenue. The restaurant's decor featured its namesake Rose Du Barry damask wall panels beneath an upper-wall frieze depicting female figures playing musical instruments by artist C.Y. Turner. Offering a menu of French cordon bleu specialties, the Rose Room became the exclusive caravansary of Fifth Avenue socialites and the hotel's most distinguished guests, courtesy of Oscar of the Waldorf and a reserved-seating-only policy. (Courtesy of Princeton University Library.)

OSCAR OF THE WALDORF (1866–1950). From the day the Waldorf opened in 1893 until his retirement 50 years later, Oscar Tschirky, universally known as "Oscar of the Waldorf," served as maître d'hôtel of both Waldorf Astorias, field marshal of the hotel's endless campaign to provide the finest in epicurean dishes and most impeccable level of service that made the hotel famous throughout the civilized world. Working 18-hour days and supervising a staff of 26 headwaiters, 50 captains, and 600 others, he oversaw every facet of the Waldorf's food, beverage, and banquet operations, from purchasing and menu planning to flower arrangements and party favors. He also served as the Waldorf Astoria's public face, greeting the arriving guests and seeing to it that their every need was met. Be they titled Europeans, New York socialites, or Texas oil millionaires, nothing so endeared the Waldorf-Astoria to its patrons as having Oscar of the Waldorf remember their names, the vintage of their favorite wine, or their preferred table in the Rose Room or Palm Garden. (Courtesy of Waldorf Astoria Archives.)

ASTORIA GENTLEMEN'S CAFÉ. Like its Waldorf predecessor, this carved-oak and stained-glass chamber was redolent with the prosperous feel of a private club. Its bill of fare leaned heavily toward robust beef, pork, and game meats, plus a few German specialties like bratwurst and sauerbraten. When this room opened, the former Gentlemen's Café in the Waldorf was transformed into a library called the Red Room. (Courtesy Princeton University Library.)

ASTORIA GENTLEMEN'S BAR. Across Peacock Alley from the Gentlemen's Café, here George Boldt abandoned his previous stance against stand-up drinkers by installing a four-sided bar of Honduran mahogany and a nearby free lunch counter. Staffed by eight bartenders and graced with bronze statuettes of a bull and a bear, the Astoria's Bar became quite popular as a place for Wall Street speculators to congregate following the stock market closing. Known collectively as "the Waldorf Crowd," such well-known financiers as J.P. Morgan, Henry Clay Frick, Charles M. Schwab, Elbert Gary, and John W. Gates convened over cigars and rye whiskey to plot the formation of the US Steel Corporation and other monopolies. (Courtesy of Library of Congress.)

JOHN W. "BET-A-MILLION" GATES (1855–1911). One of the Waldorf-Astoria's best-known permanent residents, John W. Gates (seen with a cigar on the right) and his wife moved into the hotel in 1894. As one of Wall Street's most flamboyant speculators, he created a virtual monopoly in the manufacture of barbed wire, which he then merged with several other companies to form the US Steel Corporation. An inveterate gambler, Gates bet not only on stocks and monopolies, but also on horse races, boxing matches, and high-stakes poker games, which he hosted in the Waldorf's Astor family dining room. Once, he even placed a $100 wager on which of two raindrops would first slide down to the bottom of a windowpane. Gates left the Waldorf in 1907 to move into the new Plaza Hotel, of which he was the chief financier. (Courtesy of Library of Congress.)

BROKER'S OFFICE. Conveniently located next to the Astoria Gentlemen's Bar and the ubiquitous Waldorf Crowd, this office was said to handle the largest volume of after-hours trading of any brokerage house in New York City. (Courtesy of Princeton University Library.)

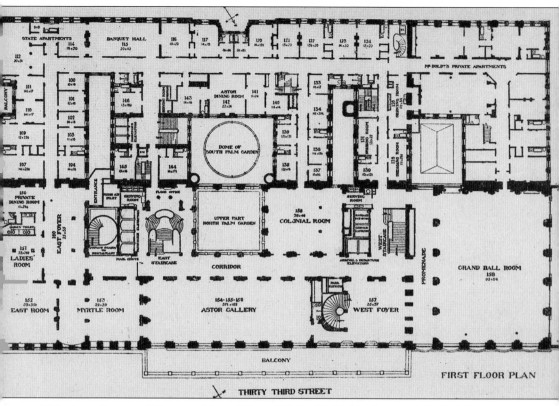

WALDORF-ASTORIA BALLROOM FLOOR PLAN. While the Waldorf's second floor plan is given over mainly to guest rooms, that of the Astoria is devoted entirely to ballrooms and banquet rooms, an indication of the hotel's increasing role as a center for New York social events. Note the "secret passage" from George Boldt's private apartment in the upper right of the plan, which was used to convey banquet honorees to the Grand Ballroom without having to pass through the hotel's other public spaces. (Courtesy of Princeton University Library.)

ASTORIA GRAND BALLROOM. Rising to a height of three stories with 43 opera boxes along three of its four walls, the Astoria's second-floor grand ballroom was easily the most spectacular of its grand public spaces. Surrounded by banquet halls and reception rooms, the white-and-gold, 10,000-square-foot ballroom was designed to serve a variety of different functions, which kept it constantly in use. The multifarious role it played was central to establishing the Waldorf-Astoria as "the unofficial palace of New York." (Courtesy of Princeton University Library.)

ASTORIA GRAND BALLROOM AS THEATER. The Astoria ballroom regularly served as a 1,500-seat theater offering "Musical Mornings" concerts by Albert Bagby and his orchestra, singing recitals by stars of the Metropolitan Opera, fashion shows, conventions, and on Sundays, religious services featuring the ballroom's Moller pipe organ. The portable stage and proscenium arch shown here reportedly could be assembled or disassembled in 30 minutes. In 1926, the Astoria Ballroom was the site of the initial radio broadcast of the National Broadcasting Company. (Courtesy of Princeton University Library.)

ASTORIA GRAND BALLROOM AS BANQUET HALL. Shown here is the ballroom decorated for a 1902 banquet honoring Prince Henry of Prussia, brother of Germany's Kaiser Wilhelm. Among the many other notables honored with Waldorf banquets were the following: Adm. George Dewey, Battle of Manila Bay hero; Gen. John J. Pershing, US Army commander in World War I (on the eve of his departure for Europe); American presidents Roosevelt, Taft, Wilson, Harding, and Coolidge; Irish president Éamon de Valera; Mexican dictator Porfirio Diaz; and Li Hung-Chang, viceroy to the dowager empress of China. (Courtesy of Princeton University Library.)

ASTORIA GRAND BALLROOM CEILING MURAL. Titled simply *Music & Dance*, Edwin Blashfield's mural was described as the largest single painted canvas ever created. Depicted in the painting are 40 individual figures, either playing musical instruments or cavorting among the clouds of a sunlit sky. (Courtesy of Princeton University Library.)

WEST FOYER. Located on the Astoria's second floor, the West Foyer served as the entrance hall of the hotel's Grand Ballroom. The circular staircase on the left led downward to the Thirty-fourth Street ballroom entrance and upward to the ballroom box tiers. (Courtesy of Princeton University Library.)

ASTOR GALLERY. One of two smaller ballrooms on the Astoria's second floor, the Astor Gallery's decorative treatment was inspired by the Rococo interiors of Palais Soubise in Paris. Along its walls were allegorical representations of the 12 months of the year by artist Edward Simmons. (Courtesy of Princeton University Library.)

EAST, OR CAEN, FOYER. Adjacent to the Astoria's guest room elevators and grand staircase from the ground floor, the East Foyer served as gallery access to the Myrtle Room, two private dining rooms, and a corridor leading to the Waldorf's State Apartments. (Courtesy of Princeton University Library.)

MYRTLE ROOM. Decorated in pale green beneath a coved plaster ceiling, the Myrtle Room was most often used as a reception room and banquet hall, with occasional employment as the setting for small tea dances. Its most famous role, however, was housing the 1912 Senate inquiry into the sinking of the *Titanic*. (Courtesy of Princeton University Library.)

SENATE TITANIC INQUIRY. From April 19 to May 25, 1912, a special subcommittee of eight US senators heard testimony from surviving passengers and crew members of the RMS *Titanic*, which struck an iceberg and sank in the North Atlantic on April 15, 1912, with a loss of more than 1,500 lives. Several press accounts of the inquiry noted the irony of the investigation into the disaster that took the life of John Jacob Astor IV being held at the very hotel he had built 15 years earlier. (Courtesy Library of Congress.)

ASTORIA ROOF GARDEN. The first New York hotel to have its own roof garden, the Astoria's Roof Garden was open during the summer months, offering refreshments and light evening suppers amid rooftop fountains and dancing to the music of two separate orchestras. Stairs at the east and west ends of the terrace allowed patrons to climb to the hotel's highest point and gaze out over the city. (Courtesy Princeton University Library.)

ASTORIA ROOF GARDEN AS SKATING RINK. During the winter months, the Astoria Roof Garden served as an ice-skating rink. Never comfortable with the idea of open-air dining, George Boldt decided to close the Roof Garden after a particularly heavy summer downpour. In the mid-1920s, new Waldorf Astoria proprietor Lucius Boomer had the space enclosed in glass for year-round, all-weather usage. (Courtesy of Waldorf Astoria Archives.)

GENTLEMEN'S AND LADIES' HAIRDRESSING ROOMS. The Waldorf-Astoria was the first American hotel to include a men's barbershop (above) and a women's beauty salon (below) among its guest services. Other hotel services pioneered by the Waldorf were telephones in every guest room and in-room dining, or room service. (Above, courtesy of Princeton University Library; below, courtesy of Library of Congress.)

WALDORF-ASTORIA FLORIST. Though the Waldorf-Astoria florist offered bouquets and flower arrangements to customers, its primary function was to create the scores of floral centerpieces used in the hotel's dining rooms and banquet halls, as well as seasonal decorations for the hotel at Christmas and Easter. (Courtesy of Princeton University Library.)

BENJAMIN FALKE PHOTOGRAPHIC STUDIO. In addition to making commemorative photographs of the various banquets and social events held at the hotel, portrait photographer Benjamin J. Falke created most of the interior images of the first Waldorf-Astoria that appear in this book from his studio located on the Waldorf-Astoria premises. (Courtesy of Princeton University Library.)

WALDORF-ASTORIA CIGAR COMPANY. In response to the era's widespread custom of concluding a fine meal with a fine cigar, George Boldt established this company to import the best Cuban cigars for the Waldorf-Astoria's male patrons. Located on the hotel's basement level, the sales room is seen in the above illustration, and at right is the humidor room. (Both, courtesy of Princeton University Library.)

WALDORF-ASTORIA KITCHEN. The Waldorf-Astoria's kitchen occupied the basement level below the two Fifth Avenue restaurants. Here, 82 chefs in three shifts prepared the meals served in the hyphenated hotel's five restaurants and banquet halls. On this level as well were the dish-washing facilities and food storage areas. (Courtesy of Princeton University Library.)

WALDORF-ASTORIA LAUNDRY. Also on the basement level, the hotel's laundry was capable of handling 65,000 pieces of bed and bath linens, tablecloths, and napkins. A separate facility for guest laundry and dry cleaning was located in the Astoria's upper stories. On the subbasement level, below the kitchen and laundry, were the hotel's steam-heat systems, hot-water boilers, and electric-power dynamos. Altogether, the basement and subbasement levels extended the building 42 feet below street level. (Courtesy of Princeton University Library.)

DISHWASHING MACHINES. Facilities for washing and storing the Waldorf-Astoria's china, glassware, silverware, and kitchen equipment were also located on the hotel's basement level. (Courtesy of Princeton University Library.)

COFFEE URNS. Cleaned on a daily basis, the seven large urns shown here were placed in the service pantries of the Waldorf-Astoria's various restaurants. The smaller urns seen in the background circulated on carts through the hotel lobbies and lounges. (Courtesy of Princeton University Library.)

Pneumatic Tubes for Visitors' Cards. Located in a corridor behind the registration desk, next to the long-distance telephone booth, these tubes sent calling cards to floor managers on each of the guest room levels who then delivered them to the individual rooms. (Courtesy of Princeton University Library.)

Three

MANHATTAN'S
MAIN STREET

For roughly a decade after its 1893 opening, the Waldorf, and later, the Waldorf-Astoria, reigned supreme as the social hub of New York. Over the next 10 years, the neighborhood surrounding the hotel changed from an exclusive residential district to a center of carriage-trade retailers. As New York's well-to-do moved to town houses and apartments farther uptown, new hotels were built to serve them: the St. Regis Hotel, at Fifth Avenue and Fifty-fifth Street; the Plaza Hotel, overlooking Central Park; and the Ritz-Carlton, adjacent to the new luxury apartment houses of Park Avenue. With such elegant establishments at their very doorstep, fewer and fewer members of the city's social elite felt the need to make the trek downtown to the no-longer-preeminent Waldorf.

Two years after George Boldt's death in 1916, financier T. Coleman DuPont and his partner Lucius M. Boomer purchased the hotel's leasehold. A master of cost accounting and operational efficiency, Boomer was ideally suited to lead the Waldorf into a new era. But then came Prohibition. Deprived of one of its most lucrative sources of revenue, the Waldorf saw its restaurants and cafés abandoned as both native New Yorkers and out-of-town visitors scurried to the city's 20,000 illegal speakeasies. Managing director Boomer took several steps to compensate for the lost wine and spirits sales: enclosing the roof garden so it could operate as a year-round facility, opening a new supper club offering dancing nightly, and most drastically, altering the majority of the hotel's Thirty-fourth Street frontage into income-producing retail space, ranging from a Louis Sherry ice cream parlor and soda fountain to the Manhattan ticket office and waiting room of the Baltimore & Ohio Railroad. Alas, his efforts could not keep up with ever-escalating costs and real estate taxes. In December 1928, it was announced that the Waldorf-Astoria had been sold and would be demolished to provide a site for the new Empire State Building. Following a grand farewell banquet steeped in nostalgia for a vanished past, the hotel closed its doors on May 2, 1929.

Lucius M. Boomer (1878–1947). Just as George Boldt had served as the guiding spirit for the first Waldorf-Astoria, Lucius M. Boomer would serve as godfather for the second. A pioneer in the scientific management of hotels and author of the standard textbook on hotel management, Lucius Boomer was the 39-year-old manager of the 1,700-room McAlpin Hotel at Thirty-fourth Street and Sixth Avenue when he was asked by T. Coleman DuPont to take over operations of the Waldorf-Astoria in 1918. For the next 10 years, he guided the aging hostelry through the difficult years of Prohibition. When the hotel finally closed in 1929, Boomer made sure to retain the rights to the Waldorf Astoria name for future use. In addition to the Waldorf, Lucius Boomer was the proprietor of the Sherry-Netherland Hotel in New York, the Bellevue-Stratford in Philadelphia, and the Willard hotel in Washington, DC. He was also president of the Louis Sherry candy and ice cream company and the Savarin restaurant chain. At the time of his death in 1947, he was serving as the first chairman of the Intercontinental Hotel Company. (Courtesy of Waldorf Astoria Archives.)

PEACOCK ALLEY, LOOKING WEST. Running between the Rose Room on Fifth Avenue and the private carriage entrance on Astor Court, "Peacock Alley" was the New York press's nickname for the long corridor along the Astoria's ground floor. Flanked by the hotel's salons, restaurants, cafés, and bar, this strip was characterized by one *New York Times* writer as "the closest thing New York had to a Main Street," a grand thoroughfare to which all came to see and be seen, including society matrons and their debutante daughters, bankers and businessmen, politicians and plutocrats, and Broadway stars and opera divas, all in a nightly display of fashion, wealth, and celebrity. (Courtesy of Library of Congress.)

PEACOCK ALLEY, LOOKING EAST. Looking east toward the Rose Room, on the right are the registration desk and the entrance to the Astoria Palm Garden; to the left are some of the retail shops installed by Lucius Boomer along Thirty-fourth Street in the mid-1920s. (Courtesy of Princeton University Library.)

READING ROOM. When the Astoria opened, the Waldorf's Bradley Martin ballroom was transformed into a reading and game room. In the mid-1920s, it became the Jade Room, a supper club offering dancing to the music of Meyer Davis and his orchestra. Meanwhile, the Waldorf's original ballroom had become a bank branch. (Courtesy of Princeton University Library.)

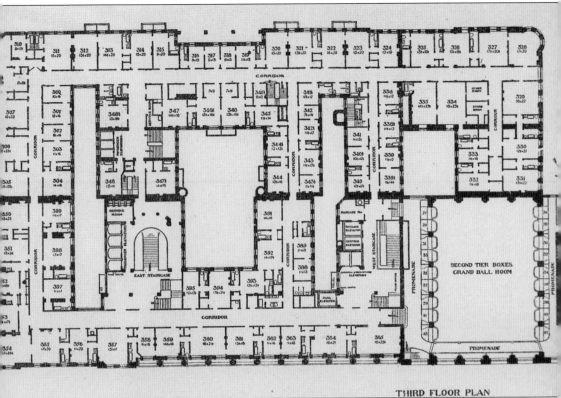

THIRD FLOOR PLAN

GUEST ROOM FLOOR PLAN. Suites occupied the Fifth Avenue corners on the guest room floors of the Waldorf and the Astoria. The larger, more costly single and double guest rooms overlooked Fifth Avenue, Thirty-third and Thirty-fourth Streets, and Astor Court, while more economic accommodations clustered around the hotel's three interior light courts. (Courtesy of Princeton University Library.)

Drawing Room, Astoria Royal Suite. The Astoria's Royal Suite was the equivalent of the Waldorf's State Suite, with a drawing room, a dining room, and a number of connecting bedrooms reserved for celebrities and foreign dignitaries—or someone willing to spend a small fortune on a hotel room. (Courtesy of Princeton University Library.)

BEDROOM, ASTORIA ROYAL SUITE. The Astoria's luxury suites were furnished with reproductions of French period pieces fashioned by the W. & J. Sloane firm or L. Alavoine et Cie. of Paris. (Courtesy of Princeton University Library.)

DRAWING ROOM, WALDORF ITALIAN RENAISSANCE SUITE. While those in the Astoria were decorated uniformly in an 18th-century French style, the Waldorf's suites and guest rooms encompassed a wide variety of period treatments. (Courtesy of Princeton University Library.)

ASTORIA DOUBLE BEDROOM. With 10-foot ceilings, the Astoria's regular guest rooms were among the largest in New York. At their registration, guests were offered the choice between brass- or wooden-frame beds. (Courtesy of Princeton University Library.)

WALDORF EMPIRE SUITE. This corner suite is decorated in the Empire style of the Napoleonic era. Both the drawing room (at right) and bedroom (below) have fireplaces, though they appear to be purely ornamental. (Both, courtesy of Princeton University Library.)

PHILIPPE BUNEAU-VARILLA (1859–1940). A French-born engineer, Philipe Buneau-Varilla had worked on France's attempts to build a canal across the Isthmus of Panama. When the French abandoned their efforts, Buneau-Varilla moved into room 1162 at the Waldorf-Astoria from which he ran a multiyear campaign to have the United States take over and complete the canal project. First scuttling the efforts to have the canal built through Nicaragua, he then encouraged American support for the revolution that separated Panama from Colombia, and finally, while serving as Panama's unofficial ambassador to the United States, he negotiated the treaty that made the Canal Zone a US territory. Thus, the Waldorf-Astoria's room 1162 may be said to be the first Panamanian embassy in the United States. (Courtesy of Waldorf Astoria Archives.)

DRAWING ROOM, WALDORF LOUIS XV SUITE. It is interesting to note that, on more than one occasion, out-of-town guests staying in Waldorf-Astoria suites asked the management if they could purchase the suite furnishings for use in their own homes. (Courtesy of Princeton University Library.)

WALDORF POMPEIAN BEDROOM. One presumes that the furnishings in this room are based on ancient Roman originals, no matter how unlikely that might seem. The divan, at least, would not be out of place at one of Nero's bacchanalian revels. (Courtesy of Princeton University Library.)

WALDORF GREEK BEDROOM. What is meant to be "Greek" about this room is mystifying, unless the moniker refers solely to the classical-styled wall murals. (Courtesy of Princeton University Library.)

WALDORF COLONIAL BEDROOM. The furnishings in this room consisted of reproductions of early American originals made by the W. & J. Sloane Company. No doubt hotel guests looking to purchase their room's furniture were advised to visit the Sloane store at Broadway and Nineteenth Street. (Courtesy of Princeton University Library.)

DRAWING ROOM, ASTORIA FIFTH AVENUE CORNER SUITE. The decor of the Astoria's Corner Suites was typically 18th-century French in style. A portion of the suite's dining room is visible through the archway. (Courtesy of Princeton University Library.)

DRAWING ROOM, WALDORF EAST INDIA SUITE. East India apparently refers to Indonesia and the Dutch East Indies. Each of the Waldorf's suite drawing rooms included an upright piano. (Courtesy of Princeton University Library.)

WALDORF STANDARD GUEST BEDROOMS. Both of the guest rooms pictured here were located in the 1896 four-story addition to the Waldorf, which contained the Bradley Martin ballroom. Their decor was more standardized than the rooms in the original portion of the hotel. (Courtesy of Princeton University Library.)

WALDORF LESS EXPENSIVE GUEST ROOM. The lower-priced guest rooms of the Waldorf-Astoria were near monastic in size but were nonetheless as fully equipped and furnished as the bedrooms of the state suites. Typically, these rooms were located overlooking the hotel's interior light courts. (Courtesy of Library of Congress.)

WALDORF-ASTORIA SHARED BATHROOM. As was common for hotels of the period, not all Waldorf-Astoria guest rooms possessed their own private bath. Shared bathrooms, like this one, tended to be utilitarian in character. The clothes hooks on the left-hand wall indicate that respective bathers came into this room and left it fully clothed. (Courtesy of Princeton University Library.)

NO. 27 TAKEN 11/7/29
EMPIRE STATE BUILDING
WEST SIDE 5TH AVE., 33RD TO 34TH STS
NEW YORK, N.Y.
VIEW FROM Southeast
SHREVE, LAMB & HARMON, ARCHITECTS
STARRETT BROTHERS, INC., BUILDERS

HAIL AND FAREWELL. Following a monthlong auction of its furnishings and fixtures, demolition of the Waldorf-Astoria began in July 1929 and was completed by that December. The 102-story Empire State Building, which rose on the demolished hotel's site, was completed and opened on May 1, 1931. (Courtesy of Avery Architectural Archive, Columbia University.)

Four

THE UNOFFICIAL PALACE OF NEW YORK

Even before the old Waldorf-Astoria had closed, Lucius Boomer made a public announcement that a new Waldorf Astoria would rise in New York. Filling an entire city block between Park and Lexington Avenues, Forty-ninth and Fiftieth Streets, the new hotel would be the largest in America in terms of its size and, at 47 stories, the tallest hotel in the world. Like its predecessor, the Waldorf's location would be in the midst of one of New York's most exclusive residential districts, the procession of luxury apartment houses lining Park Avenue north of Grand Central Terminal. Containing more than 2,200 rooms, it would provide both transient quarters for visitors to the city and apartments for permanent residents. Plans for the new hotel by the architectural firm of Schultze & Weaver called for the recreation of the old Waldorf's famed restaurants and banquet rooms, as well as a grand ballroom that, once again, would be the city's largest. The cost of building and furnishing the new enterprise was estimated at more than $40 million. Built entirely over the tracks of the New York Central Railroad, the new Waldorf Astoria would have little in the way of basement space. Consequently, its main kitchen would be located on the second floor between the ground-floor restaurants and the ballroom-floor banquet rooms. A secondary kitchen on the 18th floor would serve the Waldorf Towers residential suites. In early October 1929, it was announced that Lucius Boomer would serve as president of the new hotel, with several key personnel from the old Waldorf joining him, including Oscar of the Waldorf. The company's stellar board of directors included presidents Alfred P. Sloan of General Motors and E.W. Beatty of the Canadian Pacific Railway, magazine publisher Condé Nast, real estate developer Robert Walton Goelet, and Francis V. DuPont, the son of T. Coleman DuPont, who purchased the old Waldorf Astoria in 1918. Scheduled for completion in the fall of 1931, all indications pointed toward immediate success for the new Waldorf Astoria. Later that same month, however, the stock market crashed and the Great Depression began.

EXTERIOR OF THE NEW WALDORF ASTORIA FROM THE SOUTH. The placement of the new Waldorf's light wells and setbacks are an indication of its four interior divisions. The four-story base extending the full block holds the hotel's public spaces and function rooms; floors 5 through 17, its transient guest rooms; floors 18 to 20, private club rooms; floors 21 through 27, small transient suites; and floors 28 through 42, the 300 Waldorf Towers luxury residential suites.

Exterior of the New Waldorf Astoria from the North. Visible in this view of the Waldorf are St. Bartholomew's Church in the foreground and a corner of the Ambassador Hotel. Across Forty-ninth Street from the Waldorf is the Park Lane Hotel, also designed by Schultze & Weaver, and in the distance is the tower of the New York Central Building.

TOWER PINNACLE. The decorative twin copper-clad pinnacles atop the Waldorf Astoria house the hotel's water tanks and the electrical equipment for the elevators.

DRIVEWAY BENEATH THE WALDORF ASTORIA. A descent in grade between Park and Lexington Avenues allowed for a mid-block automobile passageway through the hotel from Forty-ninth to Fiftieth Streets. Guests arriving here by car were able to take an elevator directly to the lobby. Two stories farther below the street were a New York Central siding and platform for those arriving at the Waldorf by private railroad car.

PARK AVENUE ENTRANCE OF THE WALDORF ASTORIA. The principal entrance to the new Waldorf Astoria is on Park Avenue through six pairs of double doors beneath three large ornamented window openings, which allow natural light into the entrance vestibule and foyer. Originally, there was no marquee over the entrance, only a single canvas canopy over the central doorways, as mandated by zoning restrictions.

SPIRIT OF ACHIEVEMENT. Over the central doorway of the Waldorf Astoria's Park Avenue entrance is Nina Saemundsson's sculpture *Spirit of Achievement*. View of the statue from the sidewalk had been partially obscured by ever-larger canvas canopies that sheltered the hotel entrance over the years. When the present marquee was installed, *Spirit of Achievement* was moved forward onto it to once again place the statue in public view. (Courtesy of Waldorf Astoria Archive.)

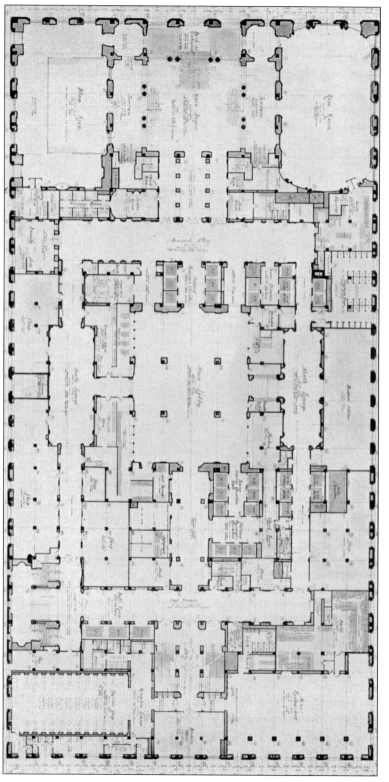

GROUND FLOOR PLAN OF THE NEW WALDORF ASTORIA. Schultze & Weaver's plan for the main floor of the Waldorf Astoria is straightforward: on the west side, the Park Avenue entrance foyer flanked north and south by the hotel's two principal restaurants, the lobby at the building's center surrounded by four corridors lined with shops, and the men's grillroom and barber shop on the east side separated by stairwells leading down to Lexington Avenue, which is at the bottom of this plan. Park Avenue is along the top.

LEONARD SCHULTZE (1877–1951). The most widely admired hotel architect of the 1920s and 1930s, Leonard Schultze spent 20 years as chief designer for the firm of Warren & Wetmore before establishing his own firm in partnership with builder-developer S. Fullerton Weaver in 1921. Schultze & Weaver designed the Biltmore Hotels in Los Angeles, Atlanta, and Miami; the Breakers Hotel in Palm Beach; and the Sherry-Netherland and Pierre Hotels in New York City.

PARK AVENUE FOYER. Up a short flight of stairs from the entrance vestibule, the two-story Park Avenue Foyer provides a formal but welcoming introduction to the new Waldorf Astoria. Sixteen paired, square columns of Rockwood Stone make up the four sides of the room, with terraces behind them on the north and south sides, providing access to the hotel's two principal restaurants, the Empire and Sert Rooms.

PARK AVENUE FOYER, LOOKING TOWARD THE EMPIRE ROOM ENTRANCE. As in the old Waldorf, the hotel's decor relied heavily on mural paintings and sculptural elements. Around the outer walls of the foyer were 13 allegorical panels depicting the gathering and preparation of food, done in a Neoclassical style by French artist Louis Rigel.

ARTIST LOUIS RIGEL AND THE WHEEL OF LIFE. Louis Rigel was also the designer of *The Wheel of Life* tapestry that occupied the center of the Park Avenue Foyer carpet. (Courtesy of Waldorf Astoria Archive.)

EMPIRE ROOM RESTAURANT. Located on the south side of the Park Avenue Foyer, the blue-and-white Empire Room quickly established itself as a favorite haunt of 1930s café society, famed for its combination of expertly prepared continental cuisine and dancing to the music of the Emil Coleman and Xavier Cugat orchestras. Renamed the Wedgwood Room in October 1941 when the room's policy changed from dinner and dancing to supper club featuring headline entertainers, it was here in 1943 that Frank Sinatra, backed by Leo Reisman and his orchestra, put his years as a bobby-socks heartthrob behind him and graduated to nightclub stardom. That same year, Danish comedian Victor Borge, recently emigrated from war-torn Europe, made his first public appearance here as a relief pianist for the dance orchestras, and quickly became a favorite with Waldorf audiences.

Sert Room Restaurant. Located opposite the Empire Room on the north side of the Park Avenue Foyer, the Sert Room received its name from a series of 15 sepia-tone murals by Spanish artist Jose Maria Sert along its walls, depicting scenes from *The Marriage of Quiteria*, a comic episode in Miguel Cervantes's epic *Don Quixote*. The Sert Room was primarily used to house private social gatherings and charity events.

Park Avenue Foyer, Looking East Toward the Central Lobby. The slender urns placed around the Park Avenue Foyer originally held the lighting units that provided the foyer's indirect illumination. Beyond the archway are the passenger elevator banks and the new Peacock Alley.

PEACOCK ALLEY. In the new Waldorf Astoria, the name "Peacock Alley" was given to a corridor-like lounge area, which guests passed through on their way from the Park Avenue Foyer to the Central Lobby. Its walls were lined with bronze vitrines displaying merchandise available for purchase from the shops in the hotel.

SOUTHERN END OF PEACOCK ALLEY. The elaborate Art Deco gates at the south end of Peacock Alley are the entrance to the Waldorf-Astoria's beauty salon.

CENTRAL LOBBY. As its name implies, the Waldorf Astoria lobby was located at the center of the ground floor, its windowless walls covered entirely with smooth burled walnut. Four large steel columns, sheathed in veined black marble and corner strips of bronze, support the weight of the ballroom on the floor above the lobby. Originally, the lobby illumination was done entirely by floor lamps; later alterations added indirect lighting fixtures around the four walls and pin spots in the ceiling. Also absent from the lobby in this photograph is the Goldsmith's Clock that currently occupies the center of the room.

GUEST REGISTRATION DESK. The hotel registration and cashiers' desks are located along the Central Lobby's south side.

ENTRANCE TO CENTRAL LOBBY. Looking westward toward the Park Avenue Foyer, one sees yet another example of the fine Art Deco–style bronze grillwork found throughout the hotel.

North Lounge. Connected to Peacock Alley at its east end, the North Lounge was intended to be lined with branch shops of some of New York's smartest retailers. When these failed to materialize, the space they were to occupy instead became the Lounge Café and Lounge Restaurant. In the 1960s, all three spaces were consolidated into the Peacock Alley Restaurant, one of the three restaurants currently operating at the Waldorf Astoria.

South Lounge. The South Lounge and East Gallery flank the remaining sides of the Central Lobby. To either side of the South Lounge's entrance to the Central Lobby are the hotel's front office and its credit department. The other side is devoted to small shops and other hotel offices.

EAST GALLERY. At the right of the photograph are exits leading to the Norse Grill, the hotel barbershop, and stairways to the Waldorf Astoria's Lexington Avenue entrance.

WALDORF ASTORIA LEXINGTON AVENUE EXTERIOR. The Waldorf's back door, so to speak, the Lexington Avenue entrance to the hotel was located between a Chemical Bank branch at the Forty-ninth Street corner and a Savarin Restaurant, not operated by the hotel, on the Fiftieth Street side. Inside, two flights of stairs brought one to the Waldorf's central lobby, with two more flights to the ballroom floor.

The Waldorf-Astoria - Norse Grill.

NORSE GRILL ROOM. Located in the Lexington Avenue and Fiftieth Street corner of the hotel's main floor was the Waldorf's gentlemen's café, where the walls and ceiling were covered with stained chestnut ornamented with carved and painted scrollwork, an atmospheric evocation of a Viking mead hall. During the day, the Norse Grill served as a strictly male preserve, but after 5:00 p.m., mixed couples were welcome. (Courtesy of Waldorf Astoria Archive.)

WALL MURAL IN THE NORSE GRILL. The Norse Grill's major decorative feature was a large painted map of Long Island showing the locations of its many famed golf, country, yacht, hunt, and polo clubs, from the West Side Tennis Club in Forest Hills to the Shinnecock Hills and Maidstone Clubs in the Hamptons.

Norse Grill Entrance Stairs. Due to the change in grade level between the Park Avenue and Lexington Avenue frontages of the Waldorf Astoria, the Norse Grill was located half a story below the main-floor level. Nestled within the curved railings of the Grill's double entrance stairs was the inevitable cigar stand.

Waldorf Astoria Barbershop. From the 1930s to the 1950s, the marble-and-chrome Waldorf Barbershop served as a tonsorial shrine for Midtown businessmen seeking a weekly haircut, manicure, and shoe shine, often followed by a leisurely lunch in the Norse Grill. A staff of 40 manned the 24 black porcelain barber chairs during the shop's heyday. By the 1970s, however, as hairstyles grew longer and less carefully coiffed, the number of chairs shrank to 12 and the staff to five.

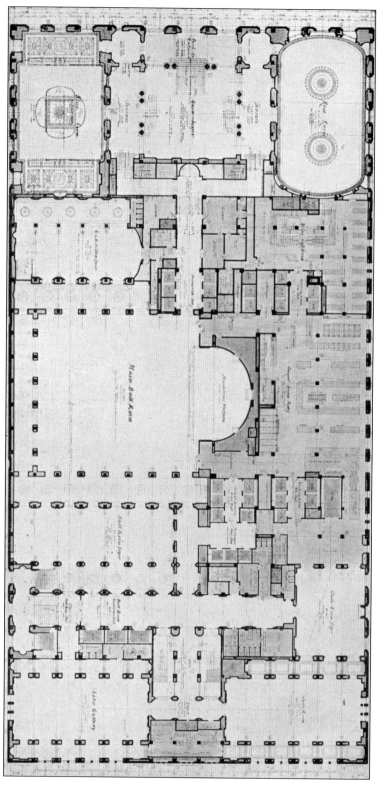

WALDORF ASTORIA BALLROOM FLOOR PLAN. Moving west to east, the Park Avenue side of the building is occupied by the upper reaches of the main-floor foyer and restaurants. The Grand Ballroom is at the center of the south side of the building, flanked east and west by foyers. The shaded area north of the ballroom is given over to service pantries and the employee cafeteria. The Silver Gallery is next to the ballroom's East Foyer and runs north to the Basildon Room. The Astor Gallery and Jade Room occupy the northeast and southeast corners of the building, overlooking Lexington Avenue, which is at the bottom of this map. Park Avenue is along the top.

SILVER GALLERY. The Silver Gallery is the central corridor between the Grand Ballroom and the three smaller ballrooms on the Waldorf Astoria's second floor. Edward Simmons's murals of the four seasons and 12 months of the year from the Astor Gallery of the old Fifth Avenue Waldorf were reinstalled here along the Silver Gallery's coved ceiling, one of the few instances of artwork from the old hotel finding a home in the new one.

BASILDON ROOM. The Basildon Room derives its name from Basildon Park, an 18th-century country house located in Berkshire, England. Architect Leonard Schultz purchased the house's Adam-style dining room interior at a London auction. The fireplace, mirrors, and wall and ceiling paintings were shipped to New York for installation in the new hotel rising at Park Avenue and Forty-ninth Street. The ceiling paintings, however, had to be modified to fit this larger interior space.

The Waldorf-Astoria - Basildon Room

ASTOR GALLERY. Recalling the name of a ballroom in the Fifth Avenue Waldorf, the Astor Gallery is decorated in a restrained 18th-century Georgian mode, with silver-gray walls, veined-marble pilasters, and rose-hued drapery. At more than 3,600 square feet, the Astor Gallery is capable of housing 250 persons for banquets, wedding receptions, and tea dances.

JADE ROOM. The Jade Room, similar to the Astor Gallery in both its function and decor, also recalls the name of a room in the old Waldorf—in this case, the 1920s supper club Lucius Boomer opened in the former Bradley Martin Ballroom. Painted green, naturally, its fluted pilasters are white marble, and its window drapes are gold toned.

Waldorf Astoria Grand Ballroom. The largest hotel ballroom in New York at the time of its completion, the four-story-high, 10,000-square-foot Waldorf Astoria Grand Ballroom could accommodate 2,000 attendees at a ball, 1,500 persons in theater-style seating, or 1,450 banqueters. The site of countless charity events, conventions, and banquets, not to mention high school proms, the annual NFL draft, and Friars Club Roasts, the Waldorf Grand Ballroom became a familiar sight to millions of television viewers who never got any closer to New York than Keokuk, Iowa.

GUY LOMBARDO, "MR. NEW YEAR'S EVE." From 1960 to 1976, bandleader Guy Lombardo and his Royal Canadians orchestra offered "the sweetest music this side of heaven" on CBS's New Year's Eve broadcast. Lombardo and his mellow saxophones playing "Auld Lang Syne" were as much a fixture of the new year's arrival as the ball dropping in Times Square. (Courtesy of Waldorf Astoria Archive.)

GRAND BALLROOM EAST FOYER. The identical East and West Foyers of the Waldorf Grand Ballroom served as reception areas for charity balls and banquets, as well as exhibition space for conventions meeting at the hotel. Modern in style, their bronze Art Deco ornament is typical of that found throughout the Waldorf Astoria.

ELSA MAXWELL (1883–1963). The self-proclaimed "world's greatest hostess," Elsa Maxwell was a fixture at the Waldorf Astoria from the hotel's 1931 opening until well into the 1960s. A fabled party thrower, she kept the hotel's ballrooms and banquet rooms humming with her well-attended scavenger hunts, barnyard parties (with live cows, pigs, and chickens), and the lavish April in Paris Ball, held annually in mid-October because that's when the ballroom was vacant. Lucius Boomer so valued her services that he gave her a rent-free suite in the Waldorf Towers. Short, fat, and frumpy, Ms. Maxwell nonetheless kept café society endlessly amused by entering the Waldorf ballroom mounted on an elephant (though rival newspaper columnist Dorothy Kilgallen expressed confusion over which was which), hosting an Astor Gallery banquet where the fish course turned out to be a pair of performing seals, attending one of her "come-as-someone-you-hate" costume soirees dressed as King Farouk, or publicly feuding for years with the Duchess of Windsor. Active well into her seventies, she was "the undisputed ringmaster of the society circus." (Courtesy of Library of Congress)

JANSEN SUITE. The fourth-floor of the new Waldorf Astoria was given over to three private dining suites intended for smaller social gatherings than those catered to by the Astor Gallery, Basildon Room, or Jade Room. Each suite included a vestibule and reception room (above) as well as the dining chamber (below). The Jansen Suite is named for its decorator, the well-known Maison Jansen of Paris and New York. The Jansen firm was also responsible for the decoration of the main floor's Peacock Alley. (Both, courtesy of Waldorf Astoria Archives.)

LE PERROQUET SUITE. Another of the fourth-floor dining suites, the Le Perroquet Suite derives its name from the exotic parrots depicted in the wall murals that adorn its dining room (above) and reception area (below). The creator of these murals, now painted over, is not identified, but their similarity to artist Victor White's murals elsewhere in the Waldorf Astoria suggest that he was responsible for them. (Both, courtesy of Waldorf Astoria Archives.)

THE STARLIGHT ROOF. Legendary is a word that can be overused even when applied to the Waldorf Astoria, but to no room is it more apt than the Starlight Roof, the Waldorf Astoria's summers-only supper club located 19 stories above Park Avenue. From its 1931 opening well into the 1950s, the Starlight Roof epitomized Gotham's elegance and sophistication through national radio broadcasts of the big bands of the era from its rooftop aerie. (Courtesy of Library of Congress.)

A SUMMER EVENING AT THE STARLIGHT ROOF. The decor of the Starlight Roof was the work of Irish-born artist Victor White, who covered its gray walls with multicolored glass mosaic depictions of sinewy trees and nightingales in flight. Overhead, the Art Deco panels of the ceiling could be retracted, allowing Starlight Roof patrons to dine and dance beneath the stars. (Courtesy of Waldorf Astoria Archive.)

STARLIGHT ROOF ENTRANCE GATE.
The detail of the principal entrance
to the Starlight Roof is seen here
decorated with Art Deco motifs.

STARLIGHT ROOF SOUTH TERRACE.
On the two terrace levels at either
end of the Starlight Roof, Victor
White covered the walls with gold-
tinted mirrored glass etched with
the same trees and birds found
throughout the rest of the room.
Staircases on the terraces led to
a balcony overlooking the room,
decorated with another etched-
glass mural by Victor White.

STARLIGHT ROOF NORTH TERRACE. The Starlight Roof measured 185 feet in length but only 35 feet wide. With their audience stretched out on three sides, some of the band singers who appeared at the Starlight Roof found it a difficult space in which to perform.

STARLIGHT ROOF OUTDOOR TERRACE. Surrounding the Starlight Roof on three sides, a seven-foot-wide balcony terrace allowed for open-air dining—a sidewalk café 19 stories above the street. The Starlight Roof is currently used to house meetings, banquets, and social events. (Courtesy of Waldorf Astoria Archive.)

XAVIER CUGAT (1900–1990). During the 1930s and 1940s, the Waldorf Astoria showcased many of the era's greatest bandleaders, but none was more identified with the hotel than Xavier Cugat. Appearing at the hotel's 1931 opening, Cugat returned to the Waldorf in 1933 to begin a 16-year run leading one of the hotel's two house orchestras. Holding a baton in one hand and his pet Chihuahua in the other, Cugat filled the Empire Room and the Starlight Roof with Latin American rhythms and soigné New Yorkers tackling the rumba, conga, mambo, and cha-cha. (Courtesy of Library of Congress.)

THE CANADIAN CLUB. Its membership made up of Canadian nationals living and doing business in New York, the Canadian Club was the largest of the social organizations housed in the new Waldorf, boasting three separate dining rooms, a library, card room, billiard room, and taproom on the 18th floor; club guest rooms and suites on the 19th floor; and an open-air terrace, handball court, and solarium on the 20th floor.

DOUBLE SIX CLUB. Its name derived from a particular type of dominoes game, the Double Six Club was a private gaming club located on the Waldorf's fourth floor. Like virtually all the club facilities once housed at the hotel, it is now used as meeting and function space.

Junior League Lounge. The Junior League of New York maintained a lavish clubhouse of its own on East Seventy-first Street. The Association of Junior Leagues International provided this 19th-floor lounge for league members visiting from other cities, who also received reduced room rates at the hotel. The New York Junior League regularly held its annual meetings and charity events at both the old and new Waldorfs.

Waldorf Astoria Men's Bar. Opened in November 1934, the Men's Bar had its own street entrance on East Forty-ninth Street and could accommodate 200 patrons in its walnut-paneled circular space. Behind the kidney-shaped bar, faced in Brazilian rosewood, are the bronze bull and bear statuettes from the old hotel. Schultze & Weaver were the architects. (Courtesy of Waldorf Astoria Archive.)

THE GOLDSMITHS CLOCK. For 116 years, the Goldsmiths Clock has chimed the quarter hour in the lobbies of the Waldorf Astorias, past and present. Created by the Goldsmiths Company of London for display at the 1893 World's Columbian Exposition, its four clock faces showed the time in New York, Madrid, Constantinople, and Tokyo beneath a miniature of the Statue of Liberty. The clock's eight-sided, gilt-and-silver base is ornamented with bas relief pastoral scenes and oval portraits of Queen Victoria, Benjamin Franklin, and six American Presidents, including Abraham Lincoln and Andrew Jackson. (Courtesy of Princeton University Library.)

Five

HOST TO THE WORLD

Grand hotels, if they are to endure, must remake and reinvent themselves to appeal to changing times, fashions, and generations. Over its eight decades of existence, the Waldorf Astoria has done just that with considerable aplomb. Built like its predecessor in what was then Manhattan's most exclusive residential neighborhood, it has seen its surroundings metamorphose from elegant apartment houses to glass-sheathed commercial skyscrapers and its café society patrons superseded by international banking and business executives and UN diplomats. Even the mighty New York Central Railroad, over which the hotel stands, is now long gone, its 20th-century Limited and Empire State Express trains replaced by the Metro North commuter service to Westchester County and Connecticut. Bereft of most of its permanent residents, the Waldorf Towers has become "a hotel within a hotel," a separate boutique caravansary catering to the wealthy of the world. Supper clubs have given way to beauty spas, men's grills to fitness gyms, live big bands to pay-per-view movies. The Waldorf Astoria itself is no longer the domain of a single visionary individual like George Boldt or Lucius Boomer; for 60 years, it has been part of the Hilton chain, its very name becoming a brand bestowed upon scores of hotels throughout the world. Some things change; others remain the same. And at the Waldorf Astoria, some changes are themselves changed and old ways restored or renewed. In this final chapter, let us recall some of the people, places, and events that have made this grandest of grand hotels "the greatest of them all."

WALDORF ASTORIA, LOOKING UP FROM EAST FIFTIETH STREET. With its own private entrance and lobby on Fiftieth Street, the Waldorf Towers occupies floors 28 through 42 of the hotel. Over the years, its luxury suites have provided quarters to a wide variety of notable guests, including Sir Winston Churchill, General of the Army Omar Bradley, film czars Jack Warner and Louis B. Mayer, and organized crime's "boss of all bosses" Charles "Lucky" Luciano.

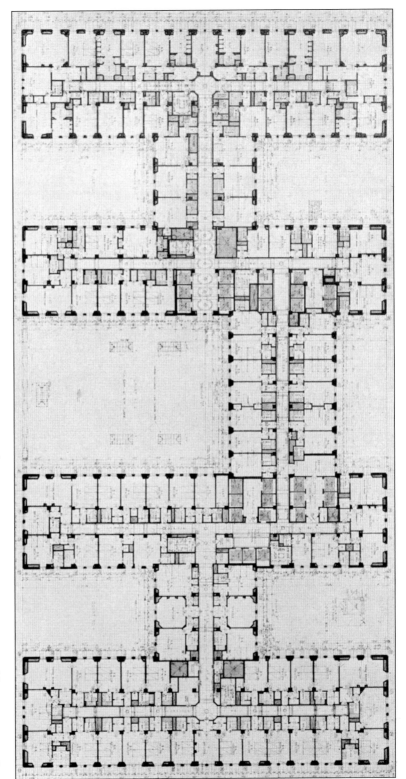

WALDORF ASTORIA GUEST ROOM FLOOR PLAN. The Waldorf Astoria's 1,500 transient guest rooms occupied floors 5 through 17 of the hotel. Single- and double-bedded rooms lined the corridors with four- to five-room suites placed at the end of the wings, overlooking Forty-ninth and Fiftieth Streets. Park Avenue runs across the top of this map, with Lexington Avenue at the bottom.

WALDORF ASTORIA DOUBLE GUEST ROOM. The Waldorf Astoria's 1,100 transient guest rooms were considered the largest in the country as well as the most elegantly appointed. In 1931, a double guest room like this one would rent for $10 to $12 a night, depending on its location.

WALDORF ASTORIA GUEST ROOM BATH. Each of the guest bathrooms contained both a bathtub and a separate stall shower. Finished in veined black marble with black-and-white tile flooring, these spaces presented quite a contrast to the Spartan bathrooms of the old Waldorf-Astoria.

WALDORF ASTORIA GUEST ROOM FOYER. Each guest room also boasted its own furnished vestibule, made to appear larger by a floor-to-ceiling mirror mounted on one of its sidewalls.

RADIO ADDRESS BY PRESIDENT HOOVER, SEPTEMBER 30, 1931. An astonishing 20,000 people came to preview the new Waldorf Astoria prior to its official opening on November 1, 1931. Speaking from the White House Cabinet Room, Pres. Herbert Hoover delivered a radio address heard throughout the hotel via loudspeakers in which he saluted the Waldorf's builders and confidently predicted that its completion signaled the beginning of a new era of prosperity and plenty. Just 13 months later, Hoover was voted out of office, and two years after that, he and his wife became residents of the Waldorf Towers. (Courtesy of Waldorf Astoria Archives.)

THE LOUNGE CAFÉ. With the repeal of Prohibition, bars once again appeared in Manhattan hotels. To the surprise of some hotelmen, women now made up a large portion of their bar patronage and had developed a distinct taste for distilled spirits. Finished in blue mirrored glass with yellow leather banquettes and a bar of tinted glass and chromium, the Lounge Café was designed to appeal to this new cocktail-imbibing clientele. (Courtesy of Waldorf Astoria Archives.)

CONRAD HILTON (1887–1979). Already the operator of the country's largest hotel chain, including the Roosevelt and Plaza Hotels in New York City, hotel magnet Conrad Hilton purchased control of the Waldorf Astoria in 1949. When asked by a reporter why he had bought the Waldorf, Hilton simply replied, "It's the greatest of them all." The Hilton Corporation is still the proud owner of the Waldorf Astoria. (Courtesy of Waldorf Astoria Archives.)

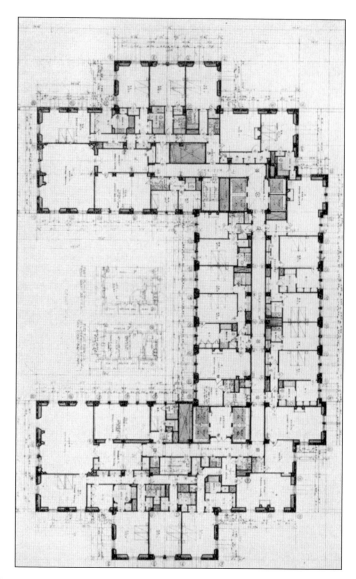

WALDORF TOWERS RESIDENTIAL SUITES FLOOR PLAN. The Waldorf Towers contained slightly more than 100 suites, about a third of which were leased as private residences. On this floor, the two largest suites occupy the south wings, overlooking East Forty-ninth Street. Eight and nine rooms respectively, not including bath, dressing, or service rooms, they each contain a large living room, dining room, gallery-like entrance hall, library/study, and four bedrooms. Two five-room suites, one four-room suite, and one of two rooms occupy the remainder of the floor, along with a service pantry, servants' quarters, four service elevators, and four private passenger elevators.

LIVING ROOM, PRESIDENTIAL SUITE. Shown here as it appeared in the 1960s, the Waldorf Towers Presidential Suite has been occupied by Queen Elizabeth II of England, Emperor Hirohito of Japan, Kings Hussein of Jordan and Saud of Saudi Arabia, Charles de Gaulle of France, Nikita Khrushchev of the USSR, and both Menachem Begin and David Ben-Gurion of Israel, as well as every American president since Franklin Delano Roosevelt. The suite contains one of Pres. John F. Kennedy's well-known rocking chairs (seen above), Gen. Douglas MacArthur's desk, and an oval mirror and table donated to the hotel by Pres. Ronald Reagan. (Courtesy of Waldorf Astoria Archives.)

HERBERT HOOVER AND DOUGLAS MACARTHUR. Seen here attending the 1980 National Football Foundation dinner, both former President Hoover and retired General of the Army MacArthur were long-term Waldorf Towers residents: Hoover from 1940 until his death in 1964 and MacArthur and his wife from the general's retirement in 1951 to his death in 1964. A replica of President Hoover's Waldorf Towers living room is exhibited at the Herbert Hoover Library & Museum in West Branch, Iowa. (Courtesy of Waldorf Astoria Archives.)

ENTRANCE FOYER, WALDORF TOWERS STATE SUITE. This is a view looking into the oval State Suite foyer through a pediment archway.

WALDORF TOWERS STATE SUITE. Located on the top floor of the Waldorf Towers, the living room (above) and dining room (below) of the State Suite, No. 42-A, were decorated in the American Colonial style by the W. & J. Sloane Company of New York. Originally the hotel's Presidential Suite, the State Suite is currently leased by the US government as residential quarters for the US ambassador to the United Nations.

COLE PORTER (1891–1964).
For 30 years, famed Broadway songwriter Cole Porter occupied a 10-room suite in the Waldorf Towers with his wife, heiress Linda Lee Thomas. Here, he wrote the scores for such musicals as *Anything Goes; Kiss Me, Kate; Can-Can;* and *Silk Stockings* on a piano that was a gift to him from the Waldorf management. Following Porter's death, Frank Sinatra and his wife, Barbara, leased his suite. Porter's piano is now displayed on the terrace level of the Waldorf's Park Avenue Foyer. (Courtesy of Library of Congress.)

DINING ROOM, WALDORF TOWERS FRENCH SUITE. L. Alavoine & Company of Paris designed this dining room with Louis XV and Louis XVI period furniture.

Lena Horne Performing in the Empire Room. Returning to its original name in 1951, the Empire Room joined the Plaza's Persian Room and the St. Regis's Maisonette as one of 1950s New York's preeminent trio of hotel nightclubs. Here in 1955, Lena Horne (in white) electrified audiences with a performance that led to a best-selling RCA Victor record album, *Lena Horne at the Empire Room*. Among other noted Empire Room headliners of the 1950s and 1960s were Harry Belafonte, Peggy Lee, Pearl Bailey, Sammy Davis Jr., Carol Channing, Ray Bolger, Ella Fitzgerald, and in his final public performances, Maurice Chevalier. (Courtesy of Waldorf Astoria Archives.)

THE DUKE AND DUCHESS OF WINDSOR. From 1938 until 1966, although their permanent residence was in Paris overlooking the Bois de Boulogne, the Duke and Duchess of Windsor would spend as much as six months of the year at their Waldorf Towers suite, No. 39-A, accompanied by a retinue of servants, private secretaries, and dogs. (Courtesy of Waldorf Astoria Archives.)

GRACE KELLY AND PRINCE RAINIER OF MONACO. On January 6, 1956, only one day after announcing their engagement, Grace Kelly and Prince Rainier made their first public appearance together in the Waldorf Ballroom at the Imperial Ball. Kelly and Rainier mounted the ballroom stage to conduct a prize raffle, he turning a drum containing ticket stubs and she drawing out the winners. Massachusetts senator John F. Kennedy won a diamond-and-sapphire ring. (Courtesy of Waldorf Astoria Archives.)

WALDORF GRAND BALLROOM, REDECORATED. In 1962, Broadway scenic designer Oliver Smith and lighting designer Abe Feder redecorated the Grand Ballroom in an 18th-century manner, changing its color scheme from a neutral cream to pale blue, with gilt detailing on the box fronts, Fragonard-like murals in the room's four corners, 16 crystal chandeliers along the upper tier of boxes, and what Feder termed a five-ton "complex of crystal" in the center of the ceiling. (Courtesy of Waldorf Astoria Archives.)

WALDORF TOWERS ENGLISH SUITE. Interior designer and antique dealer Arthur S. Vernay of New York and London decorated the living room (above) and dining room (below) of this suite in the 18th-century Georgian style.

NEW EMPIRE ROOM. In 1969, its murals removed and sold to a museum, the Sert Room was redecorated by Ellen Lehman McCluskey in the Empire style and its name changed to the Empire Room. Among the entertainers who appeared here were Louis Armstrong, Tony Bennett, Liza Minnelli, Sonny and Cher, Ray Charles, Petula Clark, Manhattan Transfer, and Mel Tormé. The Empire Room ceased operations in 1976, a victim of rising talent fees and the discotheque craze. (Courtesy of Waldorf Astoria Archives.)

THE **WHEEL OF LIFE** MOSAIC. Damaged over the years, Louis Rigel's mural *The Wheel of Life* was recreated in mosaic tile during a 1960s refurbishment of the Park Avenue Foyer. A large chandelier, a portion of which is seen in this photograph, was installed over Rigel's mural as part of the same refurbishment. (Courtesy of Waldorf Astoria Archives.)

SEN. JOHN F. KENNEDY AND VICE PRES. RICHARD NIXON FLANK NEW YORK CARDINAL SPELLMAN. Named in honor of former New York governor and 1928 presidential candidate Al Smith, the Al Smith Foundation Dinner, held in October and sponsored by the Catholic Archdiocese of New York, has marked the final joint appearance of the Republican and Democratic presidential candidates prior to the November election since 1960. (Courtesy of Waldorf Astoria Archives.)

BULL & BEAR BAR. In 1960, the Men's Bar was enlarged and redecorated to become the Bull & Bear Bar and Steak House. A new four-sided bar with the familiar bull and bear statuettes on display preserves the room's tradition as an after-market closing gathering place. (Courtesy of Library of Congress.)

BULL & BEAR STEAK HOUSE. The creation of the Bull & Bear Steak House was the Waldorf Astoria's response to the transformation of its surrounding neighborhood from one of posh Park Avenue apartment houses to corporate office buildings and banking establishments. With its own street entrance on Forty-ninth Street, the new Bull & Bear was to become a popular luncheon spot for the business executives who toiled in the glass-sheathed towers. (Courtesy of Library of Congress.)

BULL & BEAR SHIP ROOM. The Ship Room was a private dining area within the Bull & Bear used for sales meetings and banquets. Now known as the Wine Room, it continues to serve this function for the Waldorf Astoria's corporate neighbors. The Bull & Bear Steak House is one of the three restaurants currently operated by the Waldorf Astoria. (Courtesy of Library of Congress.)

SWEDISH SUITE. Jorgine Boomer, the Norwegian-born wife of Waldorf-Astoria managing director Lucius Boomer, was influential in having Stockholm's largest department store, Nordiska Kompaniet, commissioned to design this suite in contemporary Swedish style. The living room is shown above and the dining room below.

WALDORFKELLER. In the early 1960s, the hotel briefly operated the Waldorfkeller, featuring German songstress Greta Keller and a menu of bratwurst, Wiener schnitzel, sauerkraut, and beer in an atmosphere one critic described as "Hansel and Gretel Go to Heidelberg." (Courtesy of Waldorf Astoria Archives.)

INAGIKU RESTAURANT. There have been a number of specialty restaurants housed within the Waldorf Astoria. From 1974 to 2003, Inagiku was a Japanese restaurant located in rented space next door to the Bull & Bear. Part of a Tokyo-based chain, it was closed as a result of the Japanese recession. Another vanished restaurant, Shah Abbas featured a Persian menu but only remained open for a year, from 1978 to 1979, due to the ensuing Iran hostage crisis and the resulting public aversion to anything remotely Iranian. (Courtesy of Waldorf Astoria Archives.)

A Pair of Waldorf Towers Suite Living Rooms. Seen here are American Colonial designs by Pauline Sabin, with the assistance of W. &. J. Sloane & Company. A talented amateur, Mrs. Sabin was the wife of Guaranty Trust Company president Charles H. Sabin and a political activist in the anti-Prohibition movement.

Sir Harry's Bar. Opened in the late 1970s, Sir Harry's was decorated in a "plush African safari" mode, featuring zebra-striped wall coverings and carpeting, with bent-cane furnishings. Thankfully, the decor has recently taken a more traditional turn to walnut paneling and leather banquettes. Sir Harry's takes its name from African explorer and author Sir Harry Johnston. (Courtesy of Waldorf Astoria Archives.)

Oscar's Brasserie. The third of the three restaurants currently operated by the Waldorf Astoria, Oscar's Brasserie honors the celebrated Oscar of the Waldorf, who served as maître d'hôtel of the two Waldorf Astorias from their opening in 1893 until his retirement in 1943. Occupying the space on Lexington Avenue that formerly housed a Savarin Restaurant, Oscar's Brasserie offers such specialties as eggs Benedict, veal Oscar, and Waldorf salad at moderate prices. (Courtesy of Waldorf Astoria Archives.)

WALDORF TOWERS FRENCH SUITE. Here are an entrance foyer and bedroom designed by decorator Jacques Bodart of Paris in an 18th-century French style.

LEXINGTON AVENUE ESCALATOR. In the 1960s, an escalator was installed at the Lexington Avenue entrance to eliminate the two-story stairway climb to the central lobby. The Lexington Avenue entrance foyer now provides direct access from the hotel to the Bull & Bear Steak House and Oscar's Brasserie. (Courtesy of Library of Congress.)

ELEVATOR DOORS. Here are two notable examples of the use of Art Deco ornamental detail to embellish otherwise-utilitarian mechanical fixtures. The above image displays a door of the guest elevators on the main floor between Peacock Alley and the Central Lobby; the below image shows an elevator door in the Silver Gallery, opposite the Grand Ballroom.

EAST FORTY-NINTH STREET ENTRANCE TO THE WALDORF ASTORIA. This entryway provided direct access to the Waldorf Astoria's ballroom-floor elevators for those arriving for social events via taxicab or limousine.

SCHULTZE AND WEAVER'S NEW WALDORF ASTORIA. Chief designer Lloyd Morgan's Art Deco rendering of the hotel is pictured above. (Courtesy of Waldorf Astoria Archives.)

BIBLIOGRAPHY

Cowles, Virginia. *The Astors*. New York: Alfred A. Knopf, 1979.

Dearing, Albin Pasteur. *The Elegant Inn: The Waldorf-Astoria Hotel, 1893–1929*. Secaucus, NJ: Lyle Stuart, 1986.

Dorsey, Leslie, and Janice Devine. *Fare Thee Well: A Backward Look at Two Centuries of Historic American Hostelries, Fashionable Spas & Seaside Resorts*. New York: Crown Publishers, 1964.

Farrell, Frank. *The Greatest of Them All*. New York: K.S. Giniger Company, 1982.

Lamonica, Marianne, and Jonathan Mogul, eds. *Grand Hotels of the Jazz Age: The Architecture of Schultze & Weaver*. New York: Princeton Architectural Press, 2005.

Kaplan, Justin. *When the Astors Owned New York: Blue Bloods and Grand Hotels in a Gilded Age*. New York: Viking Penguin Group, 2006.

Lucas, Roger S. *The Waldorf Hotel, New York, New York*. Cheektowaga, NY: Research Review Publication, 1997.

Morehouse, Ward, III. *The Waldorf Astoria: America's Gilded Dream*. New York: M. Evans & Company, 1991.

New York Times Archive, 1890–2013.

Sandoval-Strausz, A.K. *Hotel: An American History*. New Haven, CT: Yale University Press, 2007.

Sutton, Horace. *Confessions of a Grand Hotel: The Waldorf Astoria*. New York: Henry Holt & Company, 1951.

"Waldorf-Astoria." *Architecture & Building*. Vol. 63, No. 8 (December 1931): 147–153, 165.

DISCOVER THOUSANDS OF LOCAL HISTORY BOOKS
FEATURING MILLIONS OF VINTAGE IMAGES

Arcadia Publishing, the leading local history publisher in the United States, is committed to making history accessible and meaningful through publishing books that celebrate and preserve the heritage of America's people and places.

Find more books like this at
www.arcadiapublishing.com

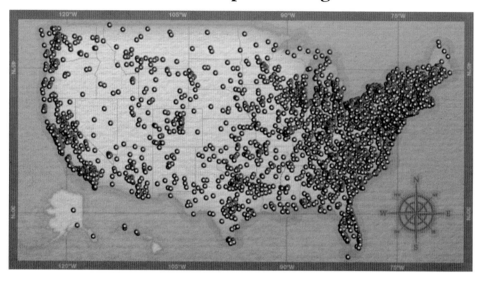

Search for your hometown history, your old stomping grounds, and even your favorite sports team.

Consistent with our mission to preserve history on a local level, this book was printed in South Carolina on American-made paper and manufactured entirely in the United States. Products carrying the accredited Forest Stewardship Council (FSC) label are printed on 100 percent FSC-certified paper.

MADE IN THE USA